OTRO / PATRIA

a collection of poems written and performed
by
.chibbi.

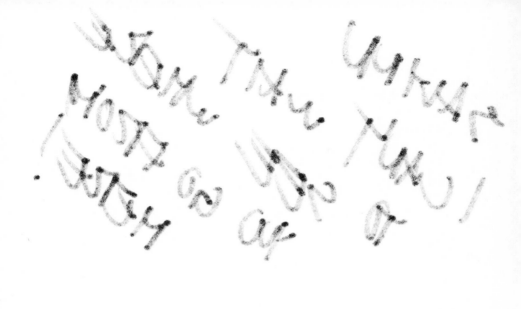

Otro / Patria
© 2019 M.Roberto Orduna
Written, designed, and published by the author
Edited with the help of Rooster Martinez, Ebony Stewart, Jennifer
Tullos, and Ryan McMasters

ISBN: 978-0-359-66031-5

Printed using Lulu Publishing Services
www.lulu.com

2nd Edition – October 2020
in the typefaces Cracked, Georgia, and Courier New

Preservation of one's own culture does not require contempt or disrespect for other cultures.
- Cesar Chavez

No quiero que pienses como yo, solo que pienses.
- Frida Kahlo

for the *OTHER* in all of us

OTRO

PATRIA

Otro

To thine
own self
be true

Pride without Community:
A *fuck you* lost
In a stampede of sheep

THE TARGET SHOOTS BACK

walking down st. mary's
at 2:30 in the morning

a group of bud light machos
in make america great again hats

let my rainbow-flag-covered-ass know
that i was a *faggot*

their spit pulled the strings
of my spine straight

eyes down mouth shut kept walking
but they—being ever so ignorant in the art of subtlety

didn't see the other cheek saw
an easy target

said it again
faggot

and i could've stayed
a shadow said nothing

hoped to just heel-click my way
to there's no place like home

like we tell women to avoid
catcalls lest they become

roadkill but how much longer will we let
a group of Jäger bombs in popped collar polos

wave their flaccid, unwelcome advances
like a get out jail free card

the status quo stroke
their misogyny on college campuses

and court rooms because silence
is permission

passive is complacent
where i come from

faggot
is a fighting word

i may be a faggot, but i ain't your faggot
i was silent in middle school before i found my voice

said nothing in high school before i knew my history
now I brass knuckle Stonewall and swing

wonder *where would I be without bloody knuckles*
well behaved women seldom make history[1]

and one lone loud-mouthed faggot will probably die
young I made myself a target

as vulnerable as paper
to burn like kindle

this is how the target shoots back
when invisibility isn't an option anymore

how a punching bag boxes back fear
how a slap in the face becomes a fist in the air

how a red hat looks
like a reminder

---

[1] Laurel Thatcher Ulrich

a MAGA hat killed Harvey Milk
a MAGA hat murdered MLK

and the target shot back
one bullet sparked

outrage created a riot fire
trust me I understand

the need to stay safe but what is life
if lived in darkness?

crowded closets watching
from the gallery

you are not safe
you're just next

and at what cost?
oppression?

erasure?
a bloody lip?

they were gonna do that anyway

WHOSE RIGHT?

I shouldn't be writing this poem
Some people would say I don't have the right

Confession #1
I was born in a city/with more letters in its name/than Sesame Street could sponsor/in a whole season/I held a resident alien card/so long/I wondered if eventually my skin would turn green/I can hold out a grito/like un mariachi chignon/y muevo las caderas bien sexy/como Shakira/These baby making hips do not lie/Hay un fuego adentro/a fire inside/that could only be fueled/by habaneros and carnes asadas/And yet/I could list the 50 states/in alphabetical order/faster than tequila tends to disappear/at a family reunion/But still/I shouldn't be writing this poem/Some people would say I don't have the right

Confession #2
Football and soccer/were both equally confusing to me/In high school/P.E./did not stand for Physical Education/but rather/Painfully Excruciating/But/I could still kick your ass–/at Mortal Kombat/so long as you let me be/Sub-Zero.../But nobody wanted to be known as the guy/that got his ass kicked by a *fag*/so I can see why you'd think/I shouldn't be writing this poem/Why you'd think/I don't have the right

Confession #3: I
struggled getting
through church
/didn't believe
that I could
search for God if I
was sitting still
/ Once, I
thought I found God/I am not kidding/in the Spice
Girls/maybe it was their individuality that made them so
universal/Maybe I thought/*This is what God must be
like*/So unique and diverse that everyone/no matter who
they are/sees their image in God and God
in their image/I
see God in
everybody/And
usually I take God
home at the end
of the night/And
he is always
beautiful /And we
find God
together/And God
damnit /They
cannot tell us that
we are wrong/But
they are still
telling us that we
are not right/
That I shouldn't
be writing this
poem/That I don't
have that right

Confession #4
I shouldn't have to write this poem/I shouldn't live in a state that protects bigotry and homophobia/and calls it *Traditional Family Values*/Where the right to discriminate is given precedence/over the right to life/Where the facts are irrelevant/so long as the fear is real

Houston set the example/Gave a public podium for people's private moments/Gave hate-based fear equal protection under the law/Dictated bathroom privileges/Decided *a dick is a dick no matter the dress*/Said a bathroom bully has the right to pray/and the right to prey/Who gets shot in the crosshairs/Who fires judgment/Where hate chooses to/Target/I act surprised;/I am not.

Confession #5
I shouldn't be writing this poem/My name is Manuel Roberto Orduña Carretero/I was born in Guadalajara, Jalisco, Mejico/I am gay/None of these were a *choice*/Misinformation - that's a *choice*/Manipulation of the facts - that's a *choice*/Ignorance - that casts votes/Maybe I shouldn't be writing this poem/Maybe I don't have the right/But I have been wrong enough times to know/that nobody is perfect/Seen enough places to know/everyone comes from somewhere/So if my existence and persistence offends you...I forgive you

From the waist down:
I'm gay
But from the belly up
I'm Chick-Fil-A, bitch!

ORAL FIXATION

There is a boy with a poem you need to hear
and it is uncomfortable.
This boy   has an erection

was called on in class and now has to walk
to the dry erase board very, very awkwardly.
He does not know why he got an erection.

Sometimes these things just happen, ok?
Maybe he got an erection because he thinks Mr. Garcia
the English teacher has a hot ass,

but this boy is uncomfortable
and probably won't admit that until many years later.
Many years later

this boy is done worrying
about making everyone else comfortable.
He will no longer be shamed into concealing

his joy
his lust
his pleasure.

This boy will proudly display his erection
for everyone to see. His poem is about
cocksucking

This poem might make you uncomfortable,
but this boy is quite comfortable addressing
the pink elephant trunk in the room.

He has a bone to pick with you:
the same 7 and a half inch bone
that picks confession and salvation

out the back of his throat.
He hums hallelujah
with communion in his mouth

to help you come to Jesus.
His poem
is titled

Mom, Don't Read This Poem

Unless Mom has a problem
with the way two individuals
show love to each other.

In which case his poem is titled
Mom, Please,
READ // THIS // POEM

Stop pretending
you're offended,
you're disgusted,

like you don't love burying your face
bush deep on the sexual organ
of the partner(s) of your choosing.

But this poem will not tell you
what to do with your body
because you have different parts or preferences.

This boy will not tell you how to worship your lover
just because we have different opinions
as to how we pray on our knees.

This boy is refusing your rhetoric.
He will not apologize for what he puts in his mouth
when you won't apologize for what comes out of yours.

Each hot coal you speak,
each commandment you spit,
every law you think will break us

Cannot compare to the strength that comes
out of this mouth,and the love that cums
in it. Say, "ahh?"

Good, you have a mouth and a tongue
and this boy can think of two things
those are good for:

orgasms and education.
This tongue can make you cum,
but let your tongue tell me

that my love is wrong,
that God didn't make me this way,
that we don't deserve your rights,

and this mouth will teach you a thing or two
and make you wish next time
you came better prepared.

This boy is a man now. This man has a husband.
Try and take that away and see if this head
don't give you whiplash.

Now if you'll excuse me
this tongue has: a poem / revolution / husband
to finish.

blindfolded, i guide
his light into my black hole
inside, he finds god

THE MOUTH OF A GODDESS

1763– london is blooming
and one in five women makes a living selling sex
all the hens come pecking when a new chicken is plucked
and here
a gaggle of geese have gathered to gawk
at the freshest bird
She spreads Her wings
full breasted and thick hipped
She has practiced each bat– Her lashes
how they whip Her eyes from side to side
as She edges   the room
throbbing with anticipation
the power
She carries in a single click of her tongue– clever
how She clucks and they come– naïve
how the rooster thinks his crow makes the world turn
it is She that gave birth to the world
it is womb that brings him to his knees
It is lips that drip with sweet satisfaction
as his purse and sack are made lighter
with his lips on hers
flushed and overflowing
She is reminded of creation
the power of the Female Flower
to make men quiver
and surrender
at the mouth
of a Goddess

4play doesn't mean 4 minutes / B4 you get 2 taste this heaven / you have to work for it 77 x 7 / leave me edging 3 inches from thirsty / like if I ain't begging for it / are you even worthy?

PRETTY GIRLS

I work as a makeup artist.
People think I sell vanity.

But my job title sometimes sounds more like:
Priest, Therapist, and Best Friend.

I see the secrets people won't tell you.
Read them in their skin.

When someone walks into my store
I cut them deep with the question:

How can I help you?
Like Josie

Josie came in about twice a week
Would ask a lot of questions and put on too much makeup

Wanted to learn how to conceal her flaws
Never had a mother to teach her how to use cosmetics

She had pain and self-doubt
She wasn't looking for makeup

She was looking for herself
Josie was a *Pretty Girl*

Growing up Josie learned

> *Pretty Girls* : Get what they want
> *Pretty Girls* : Act grown up

(bat those eyelashes, wink and smile)

> *Pretty Girls* : handle their liquor
> and their men
> *Pretty Girls* : always have a man

What's a *Pretty Girl* without her man?
> Josie thought

Pretty Girls : Shot Callers
Pretty Girls : Control

Didn't see

Pretty Girls : Handled
Pretty Girls : Dependent

Didn't realize her perception of feminine beauty
Was defined by men

Red lipstick // short skirts
Smokey eyes // hickeys

Pretty Girls
Are defined by men

Wear confidence like a Michael Kors for everyone to envy
At the end of day // discarded // vulnerable // empty

I've seen so many *Pretty Girls*
Trapped in their own misconceptions

Their happiness reliant on his
And no amount of compliments

Will ever make them believe
they are worthy alone

Josie
Walks into my store again

I ask her the same question knowing
I'll never have the right answer

GEMINI

I can tell you're busy
It's been a while since you slowed down

Hard enough to satisfy,
Harder still to love

Two minds // two hearts
I'm looking for someone to hold them both

In one hand

SUPERNOVA

Without supernovas there would be no carbon or oxygen in the universe, which means without supernovas, there would be no life.

We were both targets
Dodging traffic to hold hands in a dark theater
Communion taken behind closed doors
Sex: our only salvation

Each thrust: a middle finger to heavenly redemption
Our tongues: lashed like guilt / Our bodies: thrashed
Like war / Riding an event horizon / No tomorrow
No them / Just now / Our love

Was a protostar
At the point of nuclear fusion
Coming to the brink of burning fury
Everything else would fade away

I saw that same black in his eyes.
I question: What was he looking for?
Love? God? Himself?
The three so similar

A holy trinity of would-be answers
Written in the stars, guiding you home
If you know which ones to follow
But all he found were new ways to get lost

A Kamikaze Christ without a cause
He found bliss in the oblivion and thought:
Better to feel nothing than feel wrong.
I question: How many lips held his tongue?

Is this where he found love? In the bodies & beds
More comfortable than his own? Beside a person
We wished he could be with? Or Beside a person
He wished he could be?

I question: Where do we find God?
On the bed of a pickup truck drunk on stars?
In the arms of a stranger under the influence
Of a dance club? Barreling down a loaded syringe

Until you fall down into heaven?
And heaven looks like black tar and white china.
And heaven feels like death. And you can't get to heaven
Without dying first. And he was dying

To shed this skin he did not choose.
What parts would you be willing to cut off
In order to stitch out insecurities?
How do you know what to live with and live without

In order to live with yourself?
When pressure made you form.
When chaos made you fire.
A shooting star in the dark.

A vessel of fury and confusion.
How do you love yourself?
When the world keeps saying *Star*
but inside you feel *Supernova*

How do you accept your own death?

BORN / BECOMING / BE

Young+brown+eyes
On
the limb
of discovery look up
What a queer perspective
to find self in a wingless sky

This dis / function / ality
Norm / ality
in an abnormal world
The choice between
the bland green that feels foreign
or fly

Every action,
as ordinary as spring
The rainbow after a downpour
a promise: the pain is worth it

The heavy light
How white and dark
make brilliance

Retreat: can be healing
Isolation: a chrysalis
of neon clarity
& from it emerges the duality of
Self: What makes him different
makes him beautiful

With it, a humming confidence
His place in the world is where he's always been
In just being
nothing less
than a miracle

HOW I LEARNED TO FLY

It takes an incredulous amount
of imagination
to make steel
featherweight
even heavy souls need lifting
it takes courage
the kind they call crazy
to think Yourself worthy
of being amongst the Gods
to test the limit of what separates
Gods and men
to know
that You don't have to be half God
to fight Your demons
to know
that divinity
can be found in mortality
to not let mortality
hold You back
from Holy
to lift yourself up
to be amongst the stars
it is ok to stare into the sun
to look fear in the eye
and say,
I see you. Now step aside.
I'm going up.

HOW A HURRICANE HUMANIZES

The day the Bayou City became an ocean

Thousands lost millions

Stripped and washed clean

We found our humanity

And I pray for the day

We don't need a flood to remind us of that

Resentments and a
noose have a lot in common:

They carry dead weight

PULSE: FOR BRIGHT NIGHT BLACKOUTS

In the wake of a tragedy we have three choices:
1. We let it define us
2. We let it destroy us
3. We let it strengthen us

1.

12 years old
a girl named Samantha took my hand

I found myself looking at a boy named Hector
wondering if he wanted to take my hand too

Later I learned,
It is not ok for boys to hold hands with other boys

16 years old
I found a place where everyone was accepted

My first gay club
I had never seen people be so free

Makes me wonder
why they call them gay clubs

Wouldn't it be more accurate to call them
Don't be Afraid Clubs,

All are Welcome Clubs,
Can we Take a Minute and Admire our Differences Clubs

2.

Diversity looks dirty to some religions
Use God to justify blind faith and hate

My mother taught me
the only message God had for us was *love*

Did fear confuse you into thinking
condemnation granted access into heaven?

They keep finding ways to blackout our joy
Sometimes they use hellfire and brimstone

Other times they just fire

3.

On June 12, 2016
I hear the news about the Orlando shooting

How a *pulse*   went dead
How a nation   talked gun laws   instead

showed us   where their
priorities   lie

and it wasn't   in the victims
left lying   on the ground
of a silent   night club

My birthday is June 12th.
I will not let death overshadow the day I was born.

I mourned
and on June 13th I shined

A heart too bright for hate
too diamond to break so easily

I bleed rubies
Give C4 kisses

Love forged
under the pressure of intolerance

An existence of resistance

I will not die repentantly
I live / with pride

IN THE LAST 31 YEARS HALF A BILLION AMERICANS HAVE DIED FROM HIV/AIDS; IMAGINE IF THEY HAD LIVED TO BE 94

Michael waits in a sallow lobby. His pulse keeps rhythm with the clock on the wall, tapping his heel on linoleum floor. The color reminds him of formaldehyde: sterile, but not clean. Michael is here because it is free. A door opens. A woman walks out. Her face relieved. An apology: at the HIV clinic you can't be too happy with your good news. The next person might not be so lucky. Michael hears his number. Walks through the door.

In 1989, Michael would be one of 21,628 people to die of AIDS. That was also the year our 41st president took office. A time when the average age of death for an AIDS diagnosis was 36.

Bush lived to be 94.

I hope the ghost of your indifference haunted you on your deathbed since you couldn't care to compassion for the soon-to-be-dead. Saw the dying as less than whole. Left them behind the enemy lines of their own blood to choke on your irreverence. Did they greet you at the pearly gates? Do you see them now?

A thousand points of light[2] lost every week across America like nothing. Ignorance is a vicious killer. Neglect is serial, systematic murder. How much of a humanitarian could he be when he willfully abandoned his citizens?

America is beautiful. America is brave. America is battlefield. America is grieving. America is forgotten

I have been Michael, anxiously waiting in a sallow lobby wondering if I was positive. It has been 30 years since Michael died and I am still just as scared as he was, tapping my heel on a linoleum floor. My pulse keeping rhythm with the clock. When I get my results I wear relief on my face like an apology because you can't be too happy

---

[2] George HW Bush Inauguration Speech – 1/20/1989

with your good news at the HIV clinic. The next person might not be so lucky. I can't even say that I have been luckier than Michael. Luck had nothing to do with it. Michael was not unlucky. Michael was ignored. Imagine if he had lived to be 94. Imagine if our government had funded the research sooner. Imagine how much closer we'd be to a cure. Imagine if they saw us for what we truly are:

A thousand points of light
In a broad and peaceful sky,
Shining.

THE ALPHABET OF OTHER

When Trump campaigned on ramping up ICE raids, he
spelled out his targets for his supporters

A is for

Aliens

Amigos

B is for

Border towns

Brothers

C is for

Criminals

Caretakers

D is for

Drug Dealers

Dreamers

E is for

Enemies

Educated

F is for

Foreigners

Families

G is for

Gang members

Grandparents

H is for

Hombres

Humility

I is for

Intolerance

Idealists

J is for

Junkies

Jovenes

K is for

Killers

Kids

L is for

Losers

Luchando

M is for

MS13

Mothers

N is for

Narcos

Neighbors

O is for

Others

Optimists

P is for

Predators

Potential

Q is for

Quell

Queridos

R is for

Rapists

Resilient

S is for

Strangers

Sanctuary

T is for

Thieves

Trabajadores

U is for

Unwanted

Unidad

V is for

Villians

Virtue

W is for

Wisdom

X is for

Xenophobia

Y is for

You

Z

They only got half the lesson

LOST AND FOUND:
AN ORAL HISTORY

My birth name is Manuel Roberto Orduña Carretero. That was too many syllables for my little sister, so she called me Toto. To the rest of my family it was Manuel Roberto. That was too foreign for American integration, so I was whitewashed to Robert. That was too basic for a boy who couldn't blend in, so I became Chibbi.

But what's in a name? I was always hunting for a lost identity. Found an ancestry of lost civilizations and colonized assimilations. Aztec *and* Spaniard. Indigenous *and* Immigrant. Conquered *and* Conquistador. A hard pill to swallow having to always have to defend or destroy a part of yourself.

I found clues in my curly hair and copper skin baked in the Southern sun. The drawl of a language that walks slowly in this heat. The clipping of words when I'm fixin' to tell y'all I found out I'm a first-generation Texan.

That is what the teacher taught me in State History Class.; and I listened. When he talked about the Alamo he juggled a curriculum that clashed with his own tongue. His accent told me he's probably more a descendent of Miguel Hidalgo than Davy Crockett, but his words told me to be proud; to be grateful for those who died. The rights and privileges currently afforded to me were bought and paid for with American blood. Who was I to deny the Red, White, and Blue looming: a lone star of conquest in the corner of the classroom?

Today, I watch two sides debate the fate of lost dreamers: a modern day Alamo. Everyone claiming, *This land is my home.* Children native to this soil— uprooted. We—send a call up to heaven: *San Antonio de Padua, we pray they find their way.* And I think this is wasted breath. These dreamers are not lost. They are displaced. I find truth in their stories of a childhood of two cultures: English in the classroom and Spanish at home / tostadas for lunch and meatloaf for dinner / trying to find a balance between borders. And I come to my name, and the many places it appears: a Mexican Birth Certificate; a Resident Alien Card; a Texas Driver's License; an American Passport.

I find I am all of them, and my story of a blended experience shouldn't be the exception. For those who feel they are lost when a country tells them they don't belong; when the barrios and suburbs in the same city seem oceans apart; when those that oppress us do so despite the fact that this country was built by indigenous people and immigrants TOGETHER. Let me remind you, the blood of millions of Mexicans toiled this soil long before America Manifest-Destinied its seed on our ground, so don't tell me to go back to where I came from when this border crossed me, motherfucker.

I found my identity. It formed in the laugh lines around my Abuelo's smile. The songs my papa sings that remind me what pride sounds like. The spoonfuls of salsa on my mama's plate of migas. It passes through the mouth, lives on the tongue, of every generation of immigrants.

Identity. It isn't in our names. It is in our voice. If we don't speak it, it will be lost. If we stay silent, we don't exist.

THE UNITED CORPORATIONS
OF AMERICA

the US Constitution was written in 1787 and starts like this:

> *"We the People of the United States, in*
> *Order to form a more perfect Union,*
> *establish Justice, insure domestic*
> *Tranquility, provide for the common*
> *defense, promote the general Welfare, and*
> *secure the Blessings of Liberty to ourselves*
> *and our Posterity, do ordained establish this*
> *Constitution for the United States of*
> *America."*

a bold proclamation
    a promise of a better tomorrow
a sales pitch to the skeptical?
    do these words still ring true?
if the US Constitution was written today,
    I think it would sound more like this:

"We the People have been diminished to include only the
Elected, the accomplished to Power, powering over its
Citizens, molding these United States, in Order to form a
more perfect Profit, establish Justice that just is biased by
nature. Naturally, we must ensure Domestic Obedience,
ensuring Dependence on this system, tranquilizing
Transgressors. We provide Defense against the Common
People, and for the Companies that form our great Nation,
promoting, generally, everyone, above a certain Tax
Bracket, and abolish any Welfare that compromises the
Security of our Assets. We will continue to bless Ourselves,
and our Prosperity, ordaining this Constitution
For these United Corporations of America."

America lost its soul
to the highest bidder / left its citizens
at the base of the auction block / it happened
little by little, then all at once
while we were all watching
Big Money put Washington in its little pocket

and we   were sort of fine with that   so long as
they didn't take away My MTV   or BET
traded in Real Change for Real Housewives // News for
Entertainment // Dissent for Distraction
how could we care when we can't even C-SPAN
what's in it for me?

lost sight of the Big Picture when we swallowed that
Capitalist Pill

cuz *I was born to flex*
        diamonds on my neck
nothing in this world
        that I like more than checks![3]

                                                right?

Bad Bitches   don't wear red bottoms
                         and make money moves
Bad Bitches   wear suits and make deals
                         behind closed doors – that line
                         their pockets – make lines at food
                         pantries – unemployment offices –
                         no high-speed races just
                         \\racial divides\\

maybe Shonda Rhymes should write for CNN
then maybe we could see an end to this

                         Washington DC's basically
a lifetime of *Scandal*

                         everyone knows *How to Get Away*
with Murder

they don't pull triggers
                         they pull funding and a nation
suffers
                government shuts   down   –
                People go unpaid – Aid gets
                delayed – as a majority of
                Americans continue to slave

---

3 "Money" by Cardi B, Kelnord Raphael, Anthony White, Jorden Thorpe, Pardison Fontaine

away – at a job they hate – as the
Rich get paid – and the rest of
US get debt:
do I have your attention yet?
are you not entertained?
'cuz this show gets
renewed for
another
season
every
four
years

THE AMERICAN DREAM

Oh say can you see
by the bombs and the bills
how proudly we kill
those that stand in our way

We came here in search of the American dream
Immigrants looking for a better life
We're lining up for a seat at the table
Dying for a piece of that pie
Hoping not to disappear
The greatest magic trick of all
Is the smoke and mirrors
That turns families into statistics
At the Mexican-American border

Give us your tired, your poor, your huddled masses
Just make sure they speak English first

The American dream is a community's worst nightmare
District maps and gerrymandering draw lines
Us   Them
Paint some neighborhoods in taxpayer red
Others in squad car blue

The American dream is sectionalized
Those purple mountains majesties
And amber waves of grain
Are now borders and fences

And that land is your land
This land is my land
So keep the fuck off
My goddamn property

Conflict is our nation's currency
Keeps citizens at arms with each other
While we declare war to force peace abroad
Making pieces of whole countries
It's true

The sun never sets
On American troops

And the rockets we share
With the cartels down there
Gave food for the fight
That our borders must bear

Thousands of refugees get stamped
MS13
Labeled a threat
Named invaders
When this country funded the fire
That forced them to flee

If your country has something black, or green, or gold
Anything precious you hold
Hide the brown women and children.
Patriotism
Is an occupation of your country
For the liberation of its resources
For the creation of white wealth
And the installation
Of a worldwide corporation
Run by the American dream

Oh say does that star spangled banner yet wave
over lands that were once free
and the home of our shame

DISNEY: THE MOUSE TOOK TOO MANY TEQUILA SHOTS

*In anticipation for the release of the movie now
known as* Coco, *Disney tried to trademark the
phrase "Día de los Muertos." The following is a
response poem:*

No mames cabron! Estas pero bien pendejo pensando que
tu chingadero no iba a soltar la rabia de la gran gente de
nuestro Mexico! Chale! Obviamente tienes un putero de
pinches gringos trabajando con sus cabezas adentro de tu
culo. Siéntate, siera el ozico, escúchame y veta a la verga
hijo de tu puta pinche madre!

Which is to say,
Fuck you, Disney.

Are the ashes of my ancestors worth more in America
If you can make a Halloween costume out of them?

Did you honestly think you were big enough
To copyright a culture?

Could you not see that sugar skulls were just the sapling?
The roots of my heritage fight for life

Pierce through dirt and grime
Push aside rock and immovable object

Sing that growth to the surface
Pack a trunk full of culture

Reach out wide in every direction
And bear this fruit

I am the fruit of centuries of survival
And you think you can strip away our bark

And make it digestible for a buck? I get it
This is America: cultural appropriation

Is as patriotic as misogyny, and Corporate America
Was the big pimp money-making machine behind

Abuelita Chocolate, Aunt Jemima Pancakes, and Buddha
(*Namaste* white-girl in 80 dollar yoga pants)

Disney's been poaching indigenous people since
Pocahontas: thought they could paint

With all the colors of the wind
So long as a white hand was holding the brush

But blood, religion, and heritage,
Do not come with a suggested retail value

So glad you got the memo:
Before you make a movie about a culture,

Make sure that culture has a voice in your movie

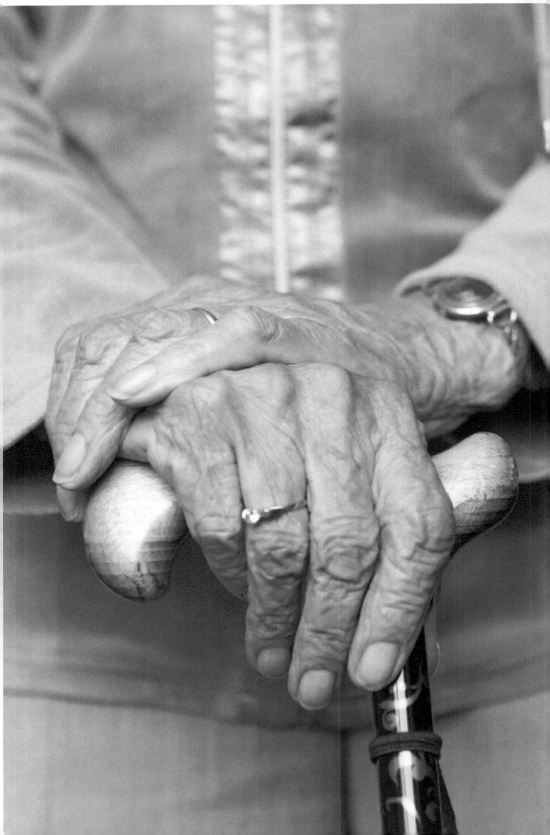

AGE OLD LOVE

Weathered hands
stories stored
between wrinkles
doughy fists
knead growth
open palms
hold hearts
cradled
no need
for white knuckle
force
secure
within their grasp
rest quietly
in the folds
where memories
bind
two lives together
a band
of gold
pales
to the riches
notched
in these hands

GRANMA: BRILLANTE

I love you
Those were never easy words for me to say
Love was never easy for me to do
I should have paid more attention
To the person you are

The first time I told you
This is my boyfriend
I was looking for discomfort
A hesitating step
A twitch in your brow
But the only movement
You made:
The   spreading of your   arms
The   widening   of your   smile
The   opening   of   your   heart

Eres un pilar de amor

You are an inspiration
You have embodied your life
Fearlessly
Brass and Bold
Como el águila de nuestro gran Mexico
You have seen so much of this world
Nurtured so many lives
I do not understand how humility
Lives with pride
In such beautiful balance

I believe in you
I believe
That we were made family for a reason
I believe
That there is no reason to be scared
I believe
That you are always with me
Like this heart
This river that flows through my veins
Eres el idioma de mi corazón

You are the language my heart speaks
and the reason we continue to grow

You are light
You have been there from the beginning
Shine on, mi Granma
Brilla

SALSA

There's a reason they call it   salsa
To watch her   cook
It's a dance
                      That couldn't be choreographed
            If you do it right
You feel it   in your hips
Each spice a step-
          two-
             three-
                four
    Slice-
       six-
          seven-
            eight

            And listen
A *pianissimo* pause
To take it in
Before she makes her next
                   ALLEGRO

To watch my mother in the kitchen
She knows   the refrain   of each recipe
But ad libs   *con apasionado*
To fine tune   each instrument   *con amore*
While there's a bass melody
She's never written it down
            She just knows
Poco a poco she relishes in   the *crescendo*
Plated   *con molto festoso*
It is always an opus
Performed   for one night only
Because, again
          She didn't write it down
Which is why I
Am eating bagel bites for the third night in a row

A SENSELESS CENSUS

Check box 1 for White
Check box 2 for White Hispanic
Check box 3 for Vete ala verga pendejo
Entitled   I am caught in the crosshairs
They ask, *What are you?*
My skin doesn't owe you anything
My skin refuses to answer

See

Underneath my skin:
My heart
Beats to the rhythm of a cannon
Each beat a command
The fight is often necessary
It is where you came from
This cannon sounds like history
Sounds like land / liberty / family
Sounds like *WISH YOU WOULD*
So I can show you what I am

> *Y retiemble en sus centros la tierra*
> *Al sonoro rugir del cañon*[4]

Underneath this heart
Is a river
Deep with wisdom
Thick
Like my Abuelo's laugh
At the dinner table
Tequila in one hand
Cerveza in the other
A smile full of stories

My river knows how to have a good time
No, this river does not divide
My river entices

---

[4] *Himno Nacional Mexicano*, written by Francisco González Bocanegra

Like pan dulce in the morning
Abuela started last night,

As she made checklists,
Changed diapers,
Made possibility,
Made a home,
Making strength seem so effortless

The pride	Se ha desbordado
A rhythm	Spread across 4 countries
A river	Underneath more than 40 temples
Call us	Holy Fortress

Amamos como los guerreros de nuestro pasado
Diamond hard truth-Open doors no matter how long it's
been-A warm meal to say *Welcome home*

Call us familia

> What I am isn't in a box
> It is in my blood

GRANMA: LO SIENTO

Querida Granma,

I want to say, perdoname. English is our second language, but it has become my first tongue, and emotions can't risk getting lost in translations. I need you to know what I mean.

I want to say, perdoname por la distancia. I'm not referring to the 987 miles of land between us, but the distance I've kept between nuestro espiritu. I'm scared. Seeing something so holy appear so fragile.

You have always been a warrior. La fuerza de los Aztecas. You carry the wind on your tongue: speak of truth, and love, and fire, and every child, and nieto, and bisnieto. With every generation your legacy becomes greater: La familia sigue. And I'm scared to accept the absence of your strength, your guiding hand, your love.

I want to say I'm sorry for the silence. My tongue tripping over the word \\cancer\\ like a sore in my throat. It has swollen y me duele hablar. Every time I try to say *I-miss-you-You-are-strong-I-love-you-You-are-inspiration-I-believe-in-you-You-are-light* I can barely breathe.

I'm sorry. Distance has made it easy to be absent. I miss you. With each passing year I grow taller, or you grow shorter, or both. Your hands reaching up to hold my face like cradles and blankets: un abrazo de Dios. And I want to hold you. Not like wheelchairs and hospital beds, but like dignity. Strength isn't measured in force. It is measured in fortitude

Maybe you need help nowadays to replace the water jug, or even open a jar, but your strength is subtle: un regalo del Espiritu Santo. It is a river after a rainstorm. La lluvia es una limpieza. Always flowing, even if you can't see it. Always present in every life around it. It lives on.

POPOCATEPETL

Virgo: Existing in the mind; everything is inside.
To the world, Virgo presents a calm and collected
exterior, but on the inside, they are nervous,
uncontrolled intensity, constantly trying to figure
things out, analyzing and thinking how to improve
everything. Virgo has a constant drive to improve
and perfect. This can lead to extreme pickiness and
finickiness, but they are pure. Their motives are
honest, never malicious.

Virgo is as honest as the earth
    I define Virgo as my sister
Upon opening her mouth
    Her words whisper up a tornado
Know that when she speaks
    It isn't just hot air blowing
It is Mother Nature letting you know
    That she has been affected

My sister is climate change
    Ignore her or put her voice
In the same box labeled conspiracy
    Defiant– she grows taller
My sister is a Virgo
    She has been fingering data like braille
She reads the signs those with sight miss
    Patient– she has been pushed
By external forces to grow
    When you meet her you can either
Stop and admire, or you can go around
    But I suggest you do the former

My sister is thought to be mountain
        The Aztecs knew better
They named her centuries ago
        My sister is Popocatepetl, meaning
The smoking mountain
        My sister is a volcano
Shrouded in Appalachian white
        So easily mistaken for cold serenity
Subterranean– a ceaseless churning of conception
        A tireless conviction to theory
Analysis   Emotion
        Her touch gives you warmth
While her tongue gives you whiplash
        Do not mistake silent for dormant
In her core she knows only
        How to give birth to fire

My sister is not the alpha or the omega
        She is the process by which this earth takes back
And builds itself anew
        A cleansing / a (re)(be)coming
She is the reason
        Islands turned into continents
Chaos made order
        My sister
My volcano
        My Virgo

LAREDO HARVEST

She was a late bloomer
Some would call her an independent thinker
Insistent in her beliefs
Isolated from far off influences
She was the daughter of two cultures
Straddling the border between
The past and the potential

She had roots that ran deep
In the Mexican culture
You could taste Aguascalientes
In the soil
In the spring
She would close her eyes and pretend
She was Puerto Vallarta
The seas of brown *monte* turned
To blue froth, tumbleweeds rolled and crashed
Like waves, the river was Veracruz and the music
Was Guadalajara
She wanted a harvest heavy in history
But light enough to stretch into tomorrow
Reap the benefits of a new land and
The possibility of a fresh start

As a kid she could cook an egg
In the afternoon sun
on the streets of Laredo
Sunday brunch con la familia
Smelled like home
Smelled like the harvest
Carne asadas and conversation
Abrazos y amor
Comida y camas para todos

She knew she could be a home for somebody
She had comfort in her routines
But her reluctance encouraged rebellion
She had to face the inevitable:
Not everyone wanted to plant seeds in her heart

How could anything grow with all that heat?
The ground steamed where she walked
Rancho, parks, and pavement alike
Memories of her youth

Those with bigger dreams than comfort
Dreams that grew like cypress
And could not be cut down
They had to fly
and she said
Ok, but don't forget where you came from.

Years later, the bodies of those entwined
In the border violence
Would be found forever sleeping on Laredo's streets
Memories of that egg sizzling lost their innocence
She had to peel flesh from stone
To lay them in dirt
Lost seeds that would not grow

The world would not let her isolate anymore
They brought camera crews and plows
They wanted to know what was buried there
They could not see the truth of who she was
They saw a foreigner

It would always be hard for her to explain herself
But I think she eventually stopped trying
To those who wanted to know, she would say
Hang out for a while.

She would invite them to walk the riverside, to see
If they could smell Veracruz or if they felt the rhythm
Of Guadalajara, or the calloused hands
Of Monterrey in her grip

Those who stayed always knew her
As Sunday brunch con la familia
An afternoon, after church, before God, y con amor

And those who left would always remember her
As the one that grew hope
The one that gave them the harvest

NAMELESS

When you have 3 pets, no carpet,
and are living your best middle class life,
for the sake of your sanity
you get a Roomba.

When we got our Roomba
we quickly named him Winston.
Christened him with a backstory:
a British butler with a drinking problem;
disgruntled but diligent

To watch Winston work he resembles
a giant, motorized, drunken hockey puck
bumping into furniture and walls.
Occasionally he would get tangled in a power cable
or trap himself into a corner of furniture.
He would let out a desperate cry for help:

```
ba buh na na...move Roomba to a new location
```

and one of us would pick him up scolding,
Damn it Winston, I told you to watch out
for the speaker cord! Pay more attention next time!

A recent Facebook post revealed
that we are not the only ones!
It seems almost every Roomba owner
has named their Roomba
AND HAS ENTIRE CONVERSATIONS WITH IT.

We do this with our pets too.
How many lonely nights have you sat on the couch
confessing to your cat
how inexplicably in love you are
with the wrong person?
Or asked your dog for financial advice?

How many of us have named our cars?
Negotiated alliances when we're late for work
and the engine won't start?

I promise to give you Premium gas next time
if you just turn on!

As a people, we are so quick to personify inanimate objects,
humanize our pets, talk to them
like they are our friends and family.

So why is it so hard
to see each other as human?

Why do we give more preference
to a poodle than a person?

Why can't we look at refugees
and value their lives more than a Honda?

We have dehumanized immigrants
to make it easier to ignore them, or worse
vilify them. Is this how we justify
importing a French Bulldog,
but deporting a Colombian refugee?

To be white in America is to have amnesia
Did you forget where you came from?
Are our differences so obscene?

If you are an American and not indigenous
by definition you {or someone you're related to}
are // an // immigrant

Your skin color may be lighter,
but your history is not so different from
the red tribes you conquered, or
the brown people seeking asylum, or
the black lives fighting for justice.

If you can have a conversation
with a vacuum cleaner
why is it so hard to have compassion
for your neighbor?

To see
it is Diversity
not Homogeny
that makes America great.

It is a black man and a Philippine woman
cooking Korean barbecue
to a backyard full of Mexicans
on the 4th of July.
That // makes America great.

That // is what makes America human:
this hodgepodge of a country we call home.

So go ahead:
name your car
name your hairbrush
name your pet goldfish.
But remember:
the people at the border
the people who have been
marginalized / vilified / ignored
they have names too.

LAS DOS FRIDAS VIVEN

*Frida Kahlo and Diego Rivera, Mexico's most
famous couple, divorced in 1939. That same year
Frida painted Las Dos Fridas, a double self-
portrait.*

A European Frida / In a white Victorian dress
Holding hands

A Mexican Frida / Wearing a traditional Tehuana costume
Hearts exposed

She bleeds out because her love cannot love all of her
80 years later Las Dos Fridas viven

The mouth / the heart: Americans cannot swallow all of me
Assimilation feels foul: cactus thorns piercing between teeth

We are asked to divorce our culture, to give up a piece of ourselves
To fit in: *Quitate el nopal de la frente*, a sacrifice

To the white god for the privilege of living \in this country\
Like Frida we bleed every time we are told to hide our accent

To only speak one language, we bleed when the features
That foreign us are seen as stains and we believe

"White-passing" is the goal, we bleed, we are told
how to look, what to wear, what to eat, who to be, we bleed

Every immigrant lives with these two Fridas inside them, one foot
On each side of the border, a balancing act of identity

[Immigrants aren't the only ones asked to edit their differences
To Photoshop themselves into the perfect picture of white America]

Isn't it funny how we paint ourselves
in different lights? How even Beyoncé

Has to bounce between being black and pop?
How even Beyoncé

Has two Fridas, but no freedom?
Code switching: a compromise to avoid persecution

We've become master manipulators of image, cropping ourselves
Into smaller and smaller boxes: be ashamed, hide from the sun

For fear of turning a deeper hue, lighter means less threatening
Same/   Equals /   Safe

\America\
thrives on bleaching color to the bone
severing a symphony down to a single note

\America\
profits from picking fruit trees clean
strips the bark off our roots

\America\
favors filters over the facts
Face-tuned skin tones and smiles

\America\
Don't we look happy to be here?
To be just // like // you?

\America\
Why are you so scared of color?
Demand varnish with bleach

\America\
Pulsing brushstrokes dissolve
Into watery scratch

Why do you want a white canvas
instead of a masterpiece?

PHOTO CREDITS

"Otro/Patria" cover – painting by Paty Orduña

"Fusion" pg. 9 – photograph by Chibbi

 "Lioness at the Reserve" pg. 18 – photo by Isabella Jusková, edited by Chibbi

"Self Portrait" pg. 25 – photo & makeup by Chibbi

"Chrysalis" pg. 29 – photo from Pixabay, edited by Chibbi

"Eye and Fire" pg. 31 – overlay of photographs by Yunus & Jose A. Thompson

"Houston Flooded" pg. 34 – photograph by Dave Einsel

"Oaxaca Sky" pg. 43 – photograph by Paty Orduña

"Cracked Flag" pg. 51 – photo from Pixabay

"Weathered Hands" pg. 56 – photo from Pixabay

"Granma" pg. 59 – photography by Chibbi

"La Bailarina" pg. 60 – etching by Paulina Carretero

"Barbed Wire" pg. 69 – photograph by Robert Hickerson

"Diego y Frida" pg. 73 – painting by Paty Orduña

"Portal" back cover – painting by Paty Orduña

FROM THE AUTHOR...

This book is 6 years in the making and there is no way I will be able to thank everyone that has influenced and helped along the way, but I'm going to try. So, thank you...

First, to my husband Cory, for always supporting me, being honest, never letting me settle, for the feedback, the love, the patience; you are my rock and my heart

To my family, all of them, the near and the far, the immediate, and the "are we even related?" for always being a source of inspiration, history, and support; specifically, to my mother for the art she lives and offers to everyone around her, and my father for always being the foundation that has allowed us to build

To the community organizers everywhere, but specifically Amir Safi, Julia Orduña, and the Write Art Out family; your work is noticed, your work is necessary, and without it works like this would not exist

To Write About Now, the space we created, the community it has blossomed, and the families that have formed are the strength that encourages and supports our work; never take it for granted; continue to nourish it, and everyone will reap the rewards

To Christopher Diaz and the 30 for 30 that never really ended, and for the joy you bring into everything you do

To Ebony Stewart, Jen Tullos, and Ryan McMasters, for the wisdom you share, the nuances you notice, and the insights you offer

And finally, to Rooster, this book would not have happened without you; the edits, the encouragement, a constant ear, a co-collaborator, the godfather of San Antonio poetry, you like to stay in the background, but I see you, I appreciate you, and I can't thank you enough.

ABOUT THE AUTHOR

Chibbi is a Mexican-born, Texas-raised poet, actor, and makeup artist. He started performing poetry in 2006 while attending the University of Texas at Austin, receiving his Bachelor of Arts in Theatre and Dance in 2009. After returning to his hometown, he founded the city's only regularly occurring spoken word competition, Laredo BorderSlam. In Houston, he was one of the founding members of Write About Now and was on their inaugural National team. He now lives in San Antonio with his husband and two fur babies, and is an active participant in the local poetry community. He was the 2017 and 2020 San Antonio PuroSlam Champion, and lead the team to a 3rd place victory at the National Poetry Slam Group Piece Competition. His work can be seen on Write About Now Poetry, SlamFind, and Poetry Slam Inc YouTube pages, and has been shared by *We Are Mitú*, and *George Takei*. *OTRO/PATRIA* marks his 2nd self-published collection of poetry, preceded by *Where the Wild Things Grow*, a journey of self-discovery as a young man explores the world on his own for the first time. He was also the co-editor of the anthology *Contra: Texas Poets Speak Out* (Flowersong Press, 2020). You can follow his adventures on Instagram @gemineyes